Tons of Trucks!

# MONSTER TRUCKS

By Luke Harasymiw

Gareth Stevens
PUBLISHING

**Please visit our website, www.garethstevens.com. For a free color catalog of all our high-quality books, call toll free 1-800-542-2595 or fax 1-877-542-2596.**

**Library of Congress Cataloging-in-Publication Data**

Names: Harasymiw, Luke, author.
Title: Monster trucks / Luke Harasymiw.
Description: New York : Gareth Stevens Publishing, [2020] | Series: Tons of trucks! | Includes index.
Identifiers: LCCN 2019011260| ISBN 9781538245170 (pbk.) | ISBN 9781538245194 (library bound) | ISBN 9781538245187 (6 pack)
Subjects: LCSH: Monster trucks–Juvenile literature.
Classification: LCC TL230.15 .H367 2020 | DDC 629.224–dc23
LC record available at https://lccn.loc.gov/2019011260

First Edition

Published in 2020 by
**Gareth Stevens Publishing**
111 East 14th Street, Suite 349
New York, NY 10003



Editor: Therese Shea
Designer: Katelyn E. Reynolds

Photo credits: Cover, p. 1 Nigel Jarvis/Shutterstock.com; p. 5 Visit Roemvanitch/Shutterstock.com; p. 7 Simon Bratt/Shutterstock.com; pp. 9, 24 (tire) Photomarine/Shutterstock.com; pp. 11, 17 BW Press/Shutterstock.com; p. 13 Maksim Shmeljov/Shutterstock.com; p. 15 Piotr Zajac/Shutterstock.com; p. 19 Neville Elder/Corbis via Getty Images; pp. 21, 24 (crush) Michael Stokes/Shutterstock.com; p. 23 Pavel L Photo and Video/Shutterstock.com.



Printed in the United States of America



CPSIA compliance information: Batch #CW20GS: For further information contact Gareth Stevens, New York, New York at 1-800-542-2595.

# Contents

This is my toy truck.
It's a monster truck!

This is a real
monster truck.
It's big!

Driven By Alan Vaughan
Slingshot
slingshot2014
CHROME
Find us on: facebook
KU06 LWB
T244 KKJ
Transport
MONTHLY

Monster trucks are tall.
They have big tires.
They are heavy.

01

Monster trucks
are many colors.
Some have names.

GRAVE DIGGER
BKT
BKT
BKT
BKT

This one is Bigfoot.
It was the first
monster truck!

LUCAS OIL
LUCAS OIL
L.A. SUPERTRUX Presents..
6
BIGFOOT

These trucks don't go on roads. You can see them at truck shows.

SPIDER-MAN
ER JAM
AB

Monster Jam is
a truck show.
The trucks do tricks!

#MonsterJam
GRAVE DIGGER
BKT

You can see the trucks up close!

Firestone
BIGFOOT
Ford
Firestone
10

Trucks drive over cars.
They crush them!

OIL
RED
DRAGON
9

I love monster trucks!

ENERGY
of FREEDOM
MONSTER MANIA SHOW

# Words to Know

crush

tire

# Index